MONSON
Free Library and Reading Room
ASSOCIATION
Monson, MA 01057

No. 68923

RULES AND REGULATIONS

Assessed fines shall be paid by every person keeping library materials beyond the specified time.

Every person who borrows library materials shall be responsible for all loss or damage to same while they are out in his/her name.

All library materials shall be returned to the Library on the call of the Librarian or Directors.

SEE ALSO
General Laws of Mass.
Chapter 266:
Sections 99, 99A and 100

The Age of the Flower

Also by Helga Sandburg

THE

Age

OF THE

Flower

POEMS

by

HELGA

SANDBURG

The Kent State
University Press
KENT, OHIO, &
LONDON, ENGLAND

Library of Congress Cataloging-in-Publication Data

Sandburg, Helga.
  The age of the flower : poems / by Helga Sandburg.
    p.   cm.
    ISBN 0-87338-501-2 (cloth : alk. paper) ∞
    I. Title.
PS3569.A48A34   1994
811'.54—dc20   93-37120
                                                CIP

British Library Cataloging-in-Publication data are available.

for Barney

Contents

Poems are autobiographical, even though one writes of the human condition. There were powerful personalities in my life. My father impressed me and I have written much on that subject. He was a prolific writer and I observed his ways and received some instruction from him regarding adjectives and the avoidance of the politics of the literary world. I adored my father.

My first two husbands were remarkable men in their ways, but I walked away from them for my own reasons. I had become involved, as I moved into my forties, in a new *raison d'être*—I was writing and making money at it. I planned on a healthy and rewarding single life. Then I encountered Barney Crile and was dazzled with love in a new way. And he—a surgeon, a traveler, and a widower—was glad to come into my arms. He was the author of a dozen books, his parents also writers. I was able to settle into a life of work, challenge, and travel, for his was a personality as powerful as my father's. Besides tremendous joy there were other events in the passage of my life with Barney, including malignancies for both of us, accidents, a stroke.

Our marriage of thirty years ended when out of the blue Barney's inoperable cancer was diagnosed. After a burst of radiation to the area, we left for Costa Rica, as he had planned. The next months were rewarding and we waited to see how long our life together would last. The ending for him was quick and merciful. My quartet of poems as a widow near the last of this book are ones that I would have liked to bring to him, as was my custom in our years together, but instead could only offer to his spirit. How fortunate I was to turn, as artists do, not to humans for solace, but to the blank page and the mind that wakes, fertile in the dark of nights, and struggles with the blessed decisive English language until the words are there on paper and the soul is assuaged of its emotion.

Helga Sandburg
Cleveland, Ohio

The Age of the Flower

Unjealous, you let me touch the flower,
Crouched kissing as if I were its lover,
Which I am, being in the power
Of all small pink roses everywhere living.

This is partly because I know the striving
That took place when all the world was greening,
When forests drowned and reptiles went sleepwalking
And no bloom was to meet a serpent's eye.

In the room's twilight their mystery
Blazes within their dark corner. The key
Is there. In the fire of the roses does lie
The answer. This is no poem but a prayer.

All Praise to the Virtue Purity

All praise to the virtue Purity!
There is no question of what it is.
It is as exact as the edge of no and yes;
It is intellectually correct man.
It is or it is not; Purity is sublime.

In Purity is no innocence;
In it is the labor of half-broken-hearted men,
Born to a martyrless time,
Not to be recognized like Savonarola tamed
On the wheel and flung on the cross
And in the Piazza burned;
Or Socrates, impatient: "What's this foolish outcry!"
To those who wept as he was starting to die.

In Purity is no excess, no indulgence, no conceit;
Purity is catholic love;
It is the hind that goes ghostly
Among the dark intertwined boles of dishonesty.

The Middle of Time

Something is happening in the kitchen there
It is not yet time for the guests to come
The woman is standing beside the dining table
He is upstairs and the quarrel has stopped ringing
Through all the house's rooms and she is beholding
What the twilight which has just struck is doing

The red wine in the vinhaber is blazing darkly
The unused polished glasses and silver glinting
The blue plates which will soon be black are burning
She cannot speak resting her hand upon a chair
Which is in ancient Greece or Persia or Rome
Or one in some far-fetched future room of the moon

The woman is stalled there in the middle of time
Which is holding still at her twilighted table
Outside the golden evening is beginning to be night
All colors not yet so soon will be colorless
The grass is glowing below the elm which gathers
Its leaves for a final burst of green radiance

The woman does not want the vinhaber emptied
The candles lit or the guests ever to arrive
Her chic dress to be passé or her emerald lost
Gift of the smoldering husband descending the stairs
Pushing the door to and coming into her arms
But their kiss is marking the ending of the twilight

In My Room Your Red Roses Are Unbeautifully Dying

In my room your red roses are unbeautifully dying!
I have been one on whom lovers at times
Have shredded red and white and rose roses in full blow;
I have been one who stood aside to watch
An uncle, wounded-eyed, tearing apart roses
And hurling them in fistfuls at his father's lowering bier.

Your red roses in the jar are too old;
When they came to my room a week ago, blushing cherubs,
I thought little of them. Now they are terrible
Reproachful angels, who stand gathered tightly
To themselves. I touch one and it trembles within
In a soft frightful way, its petals unfalling.

Your red roses in my room age before my eyes,
Mournful, black-rimmed, wrinkled as Villon's whores.
I want to throw them in the trash bin with death
And sorrow and all dark mythological emotion. Instead
I stand helpless before them, shifting my feet,
Enduring the unbeautiful dying of your red roses.

The Childe to the Tower Came

Men and countries crumble.
All things are lovely in their beginnings.
When he sat across
At that foolish German place
Outside the city (what was its name?)
And ordered small dry
Martinis, one apiece,
(Wanting later to walk in the grass by the river
And then to return to the gallery)
And *preisselbeeren* wrapped in hot thin pancakes.
In the sun-yellow window
The tables were so small one had
To push the dishes together,
And his hand kept touching because of
Being the beginning.
The gaudy-costumed waitress declared that
The president of some dark nation had been shot
And a mob had stoned the ambassador
Who was not yet dead, though near.
Her hand, freckled, trembled pouring the wine,
"Do they want independence in a day!"
The liquid spilled on the fine
White cloth, from her indignation,
In dark ochre drops.
Last week Charlemagne got thrown
Back at the gates of Saragossa (shields and stirrups clinked,
The horses' heavy coverings shifted,
And men's brooding faces gazed at the arrow-bristled walls).
The army was recalled to Saxony due to some revolt.
Now there's news of a disaster in the pass
At the narrow spot on the road from Pamplona

(They say it's but fourteen feet wide)
To St. John Pied de Port
(A thin trumpet wound the last man's falling).
"Damn the Basques, sir," our fierce
Speckle-fingered waitress cried, "when I think
Of all the dukes and Frankish chiefs slain!"
Diffident, he sympathized, "Though it's not
Our crown involved. Or our land. Now is it?
Could you please bring us cigarettes?"
The river grew dark
And the gallery had closed.
Finally because of another engagement of his
We had to leave the inn, and it
Was no longer a beginning.

The Unclasping

Did you write to me and mention love?
Love is summer. Here the foghorns roar.
Here the winter drags upon the year,
A stubborn old beast that's fastened to the throat
Of spring and will not let her go,
Will not let softness spread and change the look
Of tenseness everyone wears, mirroring desire.
Spring? It will never come. Nor love again.
The cold old lake remains a meadow of ice.
I heard in the streets that for the first time
In old men's memory the ice froze clear across.

How the winter growls and holds its grip,
While I try recalling summer and cannot.
Couples walk apart, their breath a-steam.
Was it ever summer? No. Did that pale disc
Ever boil over, pouring heat in heavy swirls
Upon the pavements of this now ice-bound town?
No. And I cannot name the name of love.
Was there ever love? No. Love is summer,
And the entire city is holding its breath,
Waiting on the unclasping of the fangs
Of winter, on the turning loose of spring.
Will you write to me again and mention love?

On War

The rain has halted which beat with wet strong wings
And we walk in the cold sweet air by our city's river.
Nature's storm is over and tongue-tied with languor,
I cannot say what I most wish to know:
Lover, what is the color of your eyes?

Darius, bloodied, died in his chariot,
Spear-riddled on that noisy plain,
In the palm of a hundred and twenty thousand Persians slain.
I hear that stinking Alexander chokes now in a drunk fever
In his fair palace; I trust he's done for.
I pray this be once and for all an ending of war!

Babylon's river flings itself in trembling gray-green tides;
The city's battlements behind us shine in dark glazed shrouds
That mirror the falling of all the empires
To the damned Macedonian commanders.
All day I can wonder only on your eyes' color.
(Women are this way; we blindly make our different pain,
Which seems small, insisting upon it with minds beyond man's
Comprehending.) The churning fumbling post-rain
Clouds above resemble battle, and in the west there,
Where yellow flare of sunset blazes, one would think
That whelp Ptolemy already had burned his path into Egypt
Or Uncle Billy Sherman's bastards swung
Their lighted pitch clubs into farmers' barns or some
Pilot struck his match to Hiroshima.

Lover, let us go home. *Your eyes at last*
Look suddenly on me! They are honeyed as the color of bees,
Green and black and amber-flecked and hot and wild and brown.
They are not yet turned away from me to the coming storm.

I Am Walking through Rooms

I am walking through rooms calling your name;
The twilight is darkening the corners;
There is nobody here, only your yellow roses;
It is raining and heat hangs like a blanket
Between me and possessions: my bed and my yellow bird
Motionless in his open cage, his shape as vague
As the shapes of your yellow roses looking
Like baby tigers. Where are you now?
I go through rooms naming your name.

Close the Door Quietly

Come in, if you will, but then leave soon.
Close the door quietly after you, please.
Don't break the silence of my rooms. I would keep
The feeling I have deep in me of trees
And grassy unconstricted places. I have been
To see my lover. It clings to me,
The luster. Tonight the faces of the stars
Will burn two degrees brighter because of it.

Don't speak, please, for I smell the breath
Of that blue-flowered weed you find sometimes
Growing tight in breasts of certain fields,
That is, if you kneel and search for it. Come in,
But go soon. Great fabled kine are lying down
In groups by woods and rain anoints their hides,
Scented, silken. Hush! I am yet struck dumb
By that rareness from which I have lately come.

Visit

In the park men doff iron broad-brimmed hats and green
Horses rear under them. Hot stone eagles scream
While overhead in a yellow despairing pool
The sun is melting. Why is it never cool
In your city! I had thought to find you alone
When I rang your bell. But that placid dark woman
Was there and would not go, spoiling it. Now I cannot return
For nearly a year. At the station I learn
That the trains are running late. In me sorrow's bud
Explodes in a slow bitter flower of finitude.

Bravery

The deep sound of your laugh has shaken me.
It broke across the evening-darkened porch,
Where sun and shade today have made their way
Through blinds and over boards; the sound came coarse
As from some old-time man, who in the noon
Walked the town streets when the Black Plague
Had frightened to death all small souls.

My conversation halted at the rough sound.
What was I saying? lost in a sudden dream of another man,
Who threw on armor to wear about his nude breast
And mounting a charger, rode to a hot brown field
Where by the time the sun had fallen in a red pool
At the end of day, he died or survived; in either case
That sound through the land broke upon the twilight.

Let Us Suffer Alone, Lover

Across the room we face each other.
You are past the tiny Czechoslovak cups of strong coffee
And the used crystal, the burned pale candles which crowd
Upon the small table draped with yellowed linen.
I am trying to tell you that I cannot be owned
Any more than you can own the tree that is in your yard
Or the dog that is in your house
Or the wife that may some day inhabit your bed.
All have their wish to be recognized by your praise,
Your command, or your hand upon her breast.
But that is enough.

We must not imprison each other.
Cut off my arms and I will run from you;
Take my legs and I will still be free;
Pluck out my eyes and close my mouth;
With your dagger spear from me my heart.
Upon my blood I shall carry my liberty
And when you have drained that you will still see
The uncrumbled wraith of me denying you.
We must release each other.
Let me go. I will return. Let us suffer alone, lover,
In the old-fashioned primeval way.

The Ballad of Woman

He took a spear and drove it in her breast.
Under her broken ribs it came to rest
Within her red and bravely beating heart.
Shaft broken, the heavy iron grew one and part
To her tamed flesh. She wore its weight so
All her victory became that none should know.

Upon a stirrup his gay boot he pressed
And bridle of his great white beast carest.
Not seeing his lady standing all in red,
He rode her down in dust of the road's bed.
When he'd gone his way she rose and washed
And returned to castle where she lightly laughed.

In her room she knelt at her prie-dieu
And all marveled at this lady's piety.

The Giraffe

Smith said, "I cannot bear to look
On that tall beast with the snakish neck
And bespeckled body. I'm feeling sick.
My eardrums throb. It's true!"

Smith did his best his courage to screw,
For he liked very much to visit the zoo.
With aplomb a fierce yellow cat he would view
And okapis bravely stare down.

But that twinkling feeble eye of brown
Was what made Smith say he'd never come
To the park again. He went straight home
And lay down, afraid. Who knows why?

Doctor, doctor, will Smith die?
That would be a catastrophe!

Dover Beach the Second

Once-love, you were not true, mark that.
It is the way I say, you were not.
If only for my loss there were a frightful cause to blame.
If, standing at the window, I could have quivering claimed,
"Fierce warring men are approaching the town gate.
You must from me run!" Alas, no, reprobate,
It was only that in your house, then mine, into white gleam
Of kitchen you'd disappear again and once again,
Emerging momentarily assuaged with plates of meat
Or bowls of things—savory, odorous, to you important.
I put up with it because you said it was marriage,
But sly-eyed, Xanthippe, the while your measure I gauged.
It was clear—the wound between you and me,
Which gaped ever wider while you forgot my beauty!

I tell it now plain. You were not true
And for this, hateless, I had at last to go
And make a room of my own where in dark gentle pain
I might build my dignity again. I am a proud woman
(Made, as women believe, for great love. The very least
Of us, cheated in her man, is convinced
Of that!). But then, there is so much, so much, yes?
Besides spouse and house, so one day one is able, no less,
To stumble suddenly up from table and confess, "Chéri,
Ta-ta. It's over the river, Socrates. You've seen the last of me!"

The Importance of Mirrors

The woman in her room is standing at the mirror.
What is she seeing? The way the wind tears her hair
As it blows through the window? No. Does she hear
Something? The cry of the old hen in the yard

Like all of them out there, from wedding card
To chopping-block, dust on their wings endured
From the leaping roosters? No. She has not heard.
Well, do her white nostrils then catch the scent

From the bedpost behind her exuding faint
(It's a virgin's cot, originally meant
For a maidenhead's taking, its boards felled luxuriant
With flowers and bees)? Does she smell it? No, nor taste

Nor feel what's physically about. She has no age, is lost
In the glass, where all her years has querying gazed
At child or wife or hag. She is the host,
Herself her guest. The mirror is her open door.

Cantata for Two Lovers

This is the way the ladies are
They are always washing and drying their hair
They are always walking into spring
And exclaiming at how long it's been
Since last year and how they've forgot the names
Of birds and flowers and other things
They are always attending to a gentleman who begs
To kneel again between their legs
And they lift their hands and put back their hair
For this is the way the ladies are

This is the way the gentlemen are
They are always in love with their mother
They are always hoping to make themselves free
And they carry swords in company
With other gentlemen who feel the same
(Though begetting sons on wives is a recognized aim)
They are always seeking to fit their hand
On a thigh which explodes above a stocking
To protect themselves from ladies they must have war
For this is the way the gentlemen are

Airmail in Summer

The summer is upon us. Lo.
In the noon streets men scarcely move;
Leaves have curled within themselves
And the insects are holding their breath.
My hand on the limp white curtain is dewed;
I don't know what book of poems I hold,
Am undesirous of sleep or love or food.
Summer is on us again. Lo.

Are you already in Italy?
I recall how the Milanese close their doors
And go to lie on beds of stone
To listen as water falls from mossy cherubs' mouths.
Above their piazzas the sun is a cauldron
Tipping slowly, as it is now doing
Here in my town. Are you yet in Florence?

Outside Arezzo, in the Etruscan country,
Past the blackbird leaning on Dante's cheek
And pigeons bathing in madonna's veils,
The wheat fields are littered with poppies!
White oxen with wilted flowers braided about their brows
Stand before the shrouded women who turn the straw
With slow forks of wood. Lo, the summer.

The hot pot of the sun boils over once again;
The heat falls thickly onto everyone.
I can nearly not move my hand through it
To my hair to push it moist from my face.
Are you planning to return by ship or air?
I read old dead poets, Vergil and Ovid

And Catullus: *What a woman says*
To an eager lover, write it on running water, on air.
Do go to see the white beasts in the evenings.
In a way I wish I were there,
For lo, here is nothing but summer.

Woman

"Will you never be done?" he said.
The woman was combing her hair.
She nodded, not stirring from where she sat;
The tortoise shell teeth in the burnished strands
Sent music forth, plucking the planets like strings
And making the moon even to sing.
So Chephren walked out on Gizeh's sand
And said he'd have a smallish pyramid built this time.
For good luck he smashed a golden cup
On his way back to her chamber.
"Will you never be done!"
"In a minute." She was in the bath;
She leaned and her knees laved with the cloth,
Then drew it up and her shoulders washed,
While butterflies spun in the sun
And in the shade a jeweled frog sung.
And Miltiades said he'd as well lead the fleet
Of seventy vessels to the Aegean to meet
The Persians and secure the Cyclades.
On his return she was pulling her stockings on,
The seams with care smoothing, one and one,
And bending to fasten the garters.
"I'll be right there,"
Her confidence such that a mountain
Somewhere moved itself somewhere else.
"Won't you ever be done?"
Hadrian made up his mind once and for all
That like Shih Huang Ti he'd build a wall;
He set one across Britain, and next made
Between the Danube and the Rhine a palisade.
And the woman on her couch was sinking,

Her fingers beneath it feeling
For her misplaced sandals.
Painters who peered through her curtains
Worked their colors like slavèd demons.
Poets listening to her sighs
Gave birth to enormous madrigals.
Successful then, toes and heels encasing,
She looped and fastened the slender lacing.
And a Child was born and crucified
And crusaders marched and empires died
And Cromwell dissolved the parliament
And slaves were freed and an atom rent,
Before she pushed the hangings and left the room,
Going to where he sat alone.
Her drew her down upon his knee.
"Are you truly done?" said he.

Am I Waiting for a Knock upon the Door?

Am I waiting for a knock upon the door?
Is it death or the next day or a friend or child I'm waiting for?
And when I hear it will I rise and lift the latch
And find no one? Will my caller be loneliness come to watch
Me stalk about my rooms? I'll draw a chair
And make him welcome saying, Oh where
Have you been? Are you afraid? You must not hide
And come more often, please. Don't remain outside
Wandering up and down the stair. I hear you sometimes in the night
And it disturbs my rest. I've often wanted to invite
You in. Do you ever stand in the shadow at the bookcase?
Am I wrong in mentioning that I've seen your face
Now that we are at last eye to eye? Have you been lost
In my mirror's dark? Now that I've found you, stay, dear guest.

Menelaus, Clytemnestra, and So Forth

AN AFFAIR

My friend is having an affair
The day is blazing
The children are shouting
There is no wind
He wants me to know he does dare
His wife is charming
Their garden blooms
A poppy is in bud
May I come and talk with you?
Suppose she finds out!
What will I do?
Powerless, my friend in his affair
The wind blows
The children have gone to bed
Careful, Menelaus

BENEFIT OF LOSS

My friend cannot speak of it.
He has lost his lover.
His eyes are like a bereaved calf's.
She sent him a letter, "It is over."

For the first time he is a poet.
See how he writes it all down.
Now he has something to bring me,
As, enchanted, he could not have done.

Sonnet about Our Neighbor's Wife

Our neighbor's wife is leaving him.
When he heard the news, he closed his ear,
He turned on his side and would not hear,
He shut his mouth upon her sin.

But she sat up in bed and said it again,
"I'll have a divorce and you can't stop me.
I'll share the kids for the alimony."
He took the pillow from his ear and said, "There's a man."

She answered in a shriek and her words were plain
And all the neighbors heard the news,
"I want to live alone without praise or abuse,
Come and go as I please minus freedom or chain."

The neighbors won't speak of it; each husband and wife
Slants glances for reassurance, terrified.

My Thief

My wallet has been stolen
And while I grieve for it
My heart goes out to the thief
Whose pleasure in this day
Is manifold for there was a
Very nice wad of twenties
Since a celebration was planned
For the man whose photo is in
The stolen wallet that the thief
Has just cast into a dust bin
And while my heart is struck
By the loss now and then
Between is the sweet happiness
I share with my thief

I'm Trying to Learn How to Die

In shadow stands primeval man,
Brute benighted, yet able to die;
In his grave: gods, arrows, meat.
No one has taught me how to die.

It's not coming war that benumbs man;
It's not science but mystery
Within himself that frightens man.
Someone should teach me how to die.

Where in our race of present man
Is someone unterrified to die?
Say you are not? I say you lie.
No use to cry, one has to die.

Tell me, is there Paradise?
Is there Hell? So when I die
There's a place to know that I can go.
I'm trying to learn how to die.

Rilke, You Gave God Back to Me

Rilke, you gave God back to me.
Dear God, you come again behind my shoulder;
I had forgot. You stand in the old proximity;
I hear you breathe, you are bolder
Than once, when you made no sound;
But then you were my doll, my plaything,
And I never felt the darkness, the wound.
How you need me! with beating wing
Rushing to see if I have called,
If I have startled from my chair,
Crying, "O, my jewel, my child,
My dear! Are you still here?"

And if you are not because you are busy elsewhere,
I make no complaint, knowing the fault of women
Is to smother love with their attentions. I require
Of you nothing. I hold my heavy white arms down
And cross them tightly on my breast so when you arrive
My tranquility and ease reassures
You that you can rest your tired head upon my love
Forever, God, needing my pity more than I need yours.

Lyric

I slept in a tomb round and red
In the land of my mother I made my bed
Until one day she set me free
And I became a devotee
Of rain and tree and earth and sky
I ran and leapt and bragged that I
Would never die but now I'm back
Within a country long and black
Awaiting another natal day
When I can again go out to play

Sometimes I Feel the Envious Dead Crowd Near

Sometimes I feel the envious dead crowd near
When the living become too much for them to endure
Longer; I sense the movement as they stir,
Uneased by so much vitality, a little pained,
In their peace disturbed, down in the counterpart land
Where they are, slow and dark, where boulders stand
For clouds, and roots repeat the patterns of our trees'
Branches, waving weighted in the netherworld's breeze,
Where under our colored flowers grow theirs like black lace.

Today a friend said, "May I come to sit in your room
And speak out—you can play your guitar—some problem
Bothering me? It's not necessary that you listen."
I felt the dead rustle then! I used once to believe
When I sensed their presences against my sleeve,
That their need for my help made them misbehave.
"What is it?" I would whisper, "is there an action undone
That I can do for you to give you rest? Have you forgotten
To take something you need?" They'd be silent again.
I have argued with them up and down for years that way,
Trying to lay them again in their own country,
Until I grew to associate them with love and joy;
Those brought them up! Like the time the shouting children
Went in spinning cartwheels and handsprings through the rooms!
"Ohhh," sighed the shades in protesting unison.

I think the most troublesome are the too recent dead,
Not yet used to the newness of eternity, somewhat afraid
Of the different landscape that is theirs now, carpeted
With slow swaying tendril roots of grass,
Balancing pebbles for bees; there are rivers that pass

Silvery in unfamiliar patterns. I want to ease
These dead, as you reason with a child
Who has lost a loved toy, "Don't look at us; in a while
You will have forgotten." They never hear my call at all.

The Cancer

Now that the fire is gone or can be argued down,
Lying beside you in the bed of our cabin
In the dawn of the morning of the operation,
Listening to the waking of April's gray woods outside,
The wild geese screaming and falling into the dark pond below
(On the island of a lake beyond, one lies like a log over eggs),
The quacking of mallards, the squeaking of wood ducks,
And the movement of my dog as he comes to stand beside my hand.

In the night the fire had risen once on waking and I had downed it,
Listening to your deep breathing in the moonlight,
Facing myself becoming a memory (not later but now).
Myself turning into a photograph, "This is how she was. You can see."
The linens in the closets disarrayed, the furniture rearranged
(A ghost, polite, I would say nothing).
Brown petals of a flower falling from a book
And no one knowing from whom they came or why placed there.
Standing at our tableside where the wine glistened
And the silver shone and the noisy arguments were flung about
(Unable to protest and enter in, being slowly erased from the scene,
Becoming a hasty flicker in the house's mirrors, uneasy of discovery
And ever so slowly withdrawing from the living).
The fire subsiding in your slow breathing in and out below the
    moon.

Now in the dawn, awake with you and ready, packing the bag, fasting.
"Put in a bottle of Scotch and the Yugoslav wine you like,"
You said from the breakfast table. We were pleased with the morning
And I pulled all the gardenia blooms for the plant's sake
And dropped them among the wine and slippers and toothbrush.
Then driving to the hospital as the sun climbed golden into the day.

Murder on the Table Top

The instant the frightful thing was done
Remorse started, violent.
My silent abrupt act had been
Devoid of any purposed intent.

The jeweled dainty-legged compact
Red spider had dashed in a sweet
Frenzy, circling the cold coffee cup. I wrecked
Its madding trip, squashed it
With a quick finger's weight.
Now it was invisible, dust.

It had not growled nor stung nor bit
And yet I dealt with it as though first
It had attacked me or meant
To do me evil in some way,
As if it were hell-sent,
Its minute size a lie.

It was a living flower.
Repentant, immoral, I quiver!

It Is April!

April: it is the season of galloping cows;
Heavy-thighed farm women are kneeling in wet fields
Tending something green and small that hides
In the brown untidy furrows. It is April!
The crooked pear tree drops white blooms.
The bull sniffs and lowers a curly-thatched head;
He digs a forehoof in the sod and roars with passion
Which arrived before he was aware and startled him
From where he cudded, lost in winter drowsing.

And the boy born in a ditch, Vergil, listens
To the white Mantuan bull, and in the distance
To springtime screaming of the Gonzaga dukes' stallions;
He leans against the budded olive tree which is a serpent,
Carvèd and still; he sighs when the air stirs;
He senses the bestiality of nearby snoring haymakers,
The suffering underlying a sun-drenched farm cottage.

And the Galilean woman in long blue robes in the crowd
Is not hearing *all* of the words of the man on the slope,
Who talks continually into a whirling perfumed wind;
She understands that he sways the people from stoning him;
She feels his limp stainèd form already in her arms,
Unfastened from the tree against the storm-rolling April sky.
The horses of the soldiers nicker in the city below,
The farmers are stripping spring-full udders of cows.

A cherry-flower touched wind sweeps down upon
The farmers' fields; there the women as if in prayer
Have fallen slowly before the sprouted seeds
In the pattern of the ages, as they always will! April.

A Short Alarming History at the Beginning of the World
Regarding Songbirds

There is a secret in the attic of birds' minds
Which has to do with scales upon their legs
They are recalling when they crawled and climbed
And like their dinosaur cousins laid their eggs

And then in order for them to survive
Their scales turned quills and icy blood grew warm
And feathers too to keep their nests alive
While all the while the wonder waited in alarm

Until the first wren fluttered and began to fly
And the tenderly-soft-voiced mourning dove to sing
And the mating reptile's bellowing croak and cry
Became the cardinal's wild sweet call in spring

Children of God

When I saw the golden glorious eyes
Of the Great Horned Owl caught in the pole trap
While raiding the farmer's wife's chickens,
I said, "It is a Child of God."

When I saw the miniature Blue Jay feather,
Iridescent in the evening sun, from he
Who destroys the singing wren's fledglings,
I said, "It came from a Child of God."

When I saw the bloodied bright striped wing
By the pasture path from a woodpecker child,
Struck down by our marauding crow gang,
Who shriek while thieving my sweet corn,
I said, "They are Children of God."

In orgiastic ecstasy over my garden
Float the mating white Cabbage Butterflies,
Terrifying the leaves below that wait for
The inevitable worms to feed upon them
And each, even the leaves, are of God.

Are these our lessons that constantly
Assail us, "All in war and peace are the
Brilliant lovely living Children of God"?

Three Serpents in a Well in a Field

Yesterday in the hot field behind our cabin,
We came upon a drying well of some other year
All grown over with crowding clover.
We pulled away the rusty iron cover
And gazed down into the gloom.

Oh mystery! Oh beautiful! Oh terror!
Three reptiles common to our countryside,
Yellow Rat Snakes, harmless constrictors,
Coiled about the ancient roped bucket
And gazed up blindly from the gloom.

Oh trinity of jewel-eyed serpents,
In whose patient veins beats the blood slowly,
Men in multitude were beheaded, maidens hurled
From cliffs in propitiation, having knelt first as we now
Over heavenly enigmas suddenly seen in gloom!

Sin

Nevertheless I killed them one and one.
It's no excuse that I was somewhat young
Or that they stole the grain in my father's barn.
As each reared its head I shot it down.
Some of them must have had nests somewhere
And some of them must have been starting to pair;
Certainly there was grain enough to share!

Their eyes were jewels, hot and black.
I looked, and innocent they looked back.
Each crossed its hands at its furry breast
And with father's rifle I did the rest.
From those days to these are long years between.
I had disremembered, but now begin to dream,
Repenting my deeds at age thirteen.

Destiny

That fatted calf, it knew. It
Heard the father's shout
And its pure knowing heart
Shrank. The running feet,
The old man's pant
Down the path unable longer to wait
For his approaching child, the downcast
Prodigal long considered lost.
The little calf against the post
Of the stall quivered, felt
The knife long before it smote
And life throbbed quietly from its snowy throat.

The Horsemen

The dead dove is falling, endlessly falling,
The bright red spot on his breast attests
To the hawk's wound from which he will never recover.

The dead men are knocking, endlessly knocking
With broken hands on the handles of the world's doors,
Which they cannot open, their lives being over.

The little children are weeping, endlessly weeping,
Fatherless, motherless, nationless, godless,
In their torn garments of darkness and no names.

The little enemy is firing, endlessly firing
Through the creaking shutters of the television screen,
A gun at someone's head, his landscape in flames.

The dove is falling! The men are knocking!
The children are weeping! The enemy is firing!
The Horsemen, the Horsemen, are riding!

The Teenagers

I saw three virgins by the road
Who had been walking in the wood.

They were sitting on a culvert edge
Underneath a privet hedge.
Their jeans and socks were ripped by a briar;
The wind had mussed their hair;
Their lipstick was all licked away.
None of them was a day
Past fifteen.
Their eyes day-dreamed,
Tear-swimming. They had
No notion why they were sad
Or why on this fine sunny day
There was nothing more to each other to say.

They looked like three nuns in a row,
Going where they had been told to go.

The Cabin

Alone, it waits for us to come and make it real,
For voices to sound, the kettle for coffee to boil.

At 6:47 on Sunday the guitar gave a shriek
As the fifth string gasped and pinged and snapped.

Silent, the cabin waits for us to come,
For doors to slam, bedsprings to creak at night.

The death smell of the mice held in their traps
Remains in the air, suggesting famine and war.

Brooding, the cabin waits for us to come.
Alone it waits for us to come and make it live.

Caging the Pipsissewa

> *Almost all the plants we found were common enough*
> *to get a specimen, or scientific voucher. The only*
> *exception is* Chimphila Umbellata, *pipsissewa or*
> *princess pine. We didn't think this tiny plant still grew*
> *here, but we found it along Pierson Creek on the*
> *steeply sloping rim of oak woods. It was browsed by*
> *deer but is now caged so it might bloom.*
> —Flora Survey, Holden Arboretum,
> Cleveland, July 1990

No longer visited by deer, whose moist muzzles
Used to nudge about her needles and roots,
The princess pine is now imprisoned
And doomed to bloom along Pierson Creek.

For the lonely rare to be guarded now to blossom,
For the bird in its gilded cage to quiver and sing,
Friends, watch out! The protective keepers are coming!
The metaphor stares at us like a living thing.

*The Romance of the Responsible Mouse
in Two Chapters*

CHAPTER ONE: DISCOVERY

It was in the kitchen drawer that the tiny turds were seen
And, symptom of pregnancy, the hot pads were quite torn,
But with respect, only two bright ones for the beautiful nest.
There was no question of my action and what was best.

I had a house to protect from gnawing teeth and full teats
And the coming hungry wee naked wriggling pink bits.
Showing the traps to our guests, "We'll give her a test.
In one bacon rind, the other cheese. Her final feast."

CHAPTER TWO: THE DECISION

It seemed so simple, so humorous, so very like a fable,
Waiting for the end of the nest and tidy little mouse lady.
Talking of her lightly with friends and taking bets
As to which of the morsels would suit her tummy least.

But then the awful day. "Oh, she chose the cheese!"
And, "Oh, the soft gray body plump with dainty babes!"
And, "Oh, murder, and the mother's mournful dark breasts
And somewhere, made of bright cotton, a waiting nest."

EPILOGUE

*The Responsible Mouse was respectful and also my guest
And I cannot make out whether this is a romance or a jest.*

The Calf of the Black Cow

The calf the black cow had inside of her
Refused to be ordinarily birthed.
He had grown grotesque within her natural womb,
Like some noble bewitched thing foredoomed.
The black cow fell upon her knees in wonder
Near midnight; the twisted rope hung from her,
Which told the farmer the channel for her young
Had opened; but the child would not come;
Heavy-skulled, furry, to the womb's walls he clung,
Through his mother bawled and in the barnyard flung.

At dawn the veterinary leaned against a tree
And aimed and spit tobacco and drowned a fly
And rolled his sleeves and his fingers greased
And the knife bent double within his fist.
Up to his bloodied shoulder in the cow
He did to death the thing which wrongly grew;
And when he went to the trough to wash his arm,
The bull calf lay dismembered on the lawn;
And from the severed monstrous curly-locked head,
Huge eyes gazed liquid, gentle, enchanted.

The black cow sighed and came to lick the face of her son,
Who had made his stand and fought his war and won.

The Accident

Forced by broken ribs to contemplation,
I thought of how it would be to be dead,
Not lying here folded in a great white bed,
But cased in a box and under a stone instead.

I thought of all my lively filaments
That now are stretched and smashed to cause me pain,
Dissolving quietly in autumn rain,
Falling apart to dust and air again.

I thought of my bones' responsiveness,
How easily they manage in my skin,
Linked by harmonious cartilage within
The fabulous frame of my skeleton.

I thought of my blood's warm tranquility,
If caught by the blow that surprised my ribs in two,
Cooling gradually to a temperature all new,
Thickening, disintegrating, until ashes too.

I thought with pride of my brain's perfection,
How it lies delicate within my head,
Convoluted, beautiful, veined red,
Wondering on how it would be to be dead.

I thought of that most innate part of me,
That unperceivable essence I admire,
And how tangibly it might not expire,
But redistribute its fine ineffable fire.

A Case of Bad Taste

Agriculture Secretary Edward Madigan says the northern spotted owl's bad taste in mates may be partly responsible for its decline in the old forests of the Northwest. There may be little the government can do to protect the bird from extinction because it is increasingly mating with the more aggressive barred owl. The offspring of such unions could not be considered a spotted owl under the terms of the endangered species act.
        —News item, July 1992

Take that, pretty spotted owl,
Haunter of the dense coniferous forests
And remote and shaded mountain canyons,
Seldom moving in the daytime,
Slumbering in your cool retreats.

Watch it, little spotted caller,
Round-faced, with no ear tufts,
With big spectral eyes, your voice
Abrupt, high-pitched and somewhat
Like a distant barking dog.

For shame, northern spotted one,
To take or be taken by another species,
A taloned raptor to boot and barred, you know,
So that your children bear the stain
And man withdraws protection of your race.

Our Agricultural Department leaders have
Sent out the word, but has the little owl heard?

The Silence

The silence in there must have been tremendous,
In that cave called *L'Aven Armand* near the Gorge du Tarn,
Not far from Roquefort and found by the Frenchman, Martel,
Who was lowered into it by a rope ladder in 1898.

The silence began while the stupendous cave formed.
A lizard went there to stay, in time blinded and deafened,
Prowling about the stalagmites and stalactites,
The only living form in *L'Aven*, the chasm, near Armand.
Over the eons mankind evolved and in time found the hole
Where curious shepherds and children and wandering lovers
Dropped stones and listened for the distant echo of nothing.

The silence was broken by the Frenchman.
The darkness was invaded by his lantern.
The lizard noted neither except the breaking of the forest
Of virgin stalagmites and stalactites by the comers.

Now there is a tramway and guides and lights and paths.
Only at night when the last guard has gone
Does silence seep back into the grotto,
Silence starting at the dead center
And meeting at the walls and returning,
Silence so profound that the only noise is the breathing
And the beating heart of the deaf blind speechless lizard.

Song for a Poetess Done In by a Bunch of Red Blooms
(in 3 Stanzas and a Chorus)

"Before they came the air was calm enough . . ."
                              —"Tulips," Sylvia Plath

The poetess is proud and damned and very fair
In the high hospital bed over there,
But the red-toothed tulips are eating her air
And she hasn't a chance to survive.

> CHORUS
> So ring the bell, the happy bell,
> Hang on the rope and toll (or knell?) farewell.
> Ding dong, comb out the long and lovely hair
> Of the little poetess so young and so fair!

Who greeted Death with a slinky smile
And asked Death to not only knock but come in awhile
And have some conversation on which tombstones are in style,
Since someone turned loose the red-tongued tulips which are
    sapping her life

(Repeat) CHORUS

The lady is sinking due to the lack of oxygen,
Which the greedy toothy tulips love and gobble with a mouthy grin.
The walls of the room are slowly closing in
And before long the little poetess will try another suicide.

(Repeat) CHORUS

49

On Returning to Egypt and Waking at the Ruins of the
Continental Savoy Hotel After Visiting Cairo's Museum and Giza
the Day Before and in the Evening Attending the "Sound and Light"
Spectacle Which Was in Incomprehensible French Although English
Had Been Promised

This morning you come to my bed after the Dream.
Your blue eyes in the sun gleam like gold.
Beyond Cairo's blaring traffic horns lie pyramids,
Which tower behind the crouched serene Sphinx.

Once here I heard beggars crying their dream,
Baksheesh-begging beggars begging gold
Their far-away ancestors had robbed from the pyramids,
While stripping the skins from them and from the Sphinx.

Last night French voices howled, "Reve!" (dream)
Norman women screamed, "Or!" (gold)
Napoleon's countrymen cried, "Les pyramides!"
And the actor roared, "Je suis le Sphinx!"

Colored lights alternated over the dream
Before the audience in rays of blue and rose and gold,
Illuminating Mycerinus' and Chephren's and Cheops' pyramids,
As well as the smaller ones and Pharaoh Sphinx.

Above Chephren's tomb as in a starry dream
A single bright planet (Venus?) shown pure gold
And plunged in the spectacle's hour to the pyramid,
While Orion kept on wheeling over the Sphinx.

I was remembering how I stood in a startled dream
Before King Tutankhamen's Chair of glorious gold
Among his treasures assembled in disarrayed pyramids
In Cairo's dusty museum, which (trust me) is a sphinx.

Nefertiti's daughter and her Pharaoh in their dream,
Her sensuous hands, his glowing face in streaming gold
From Aton, their God Sun—those three made a pyramid
Of Eternal Youth and Love and Life—a sphinx?

Now your gold eyes in my bed after the Dream,
In which I rode a dreaming camel of gold
About three gigantic golden pyramids
And then under the paws of a golden dreaming Sphinx

The camel knelt and there the smiling Sphinx
Leaned down and unriddled the riddle of the pyramids,
But all in French! Then those eyes, glowing gold
Became your eyes, waking me from the Dream.

The Visitor

Returned this year to the old tall house
Where my childhood was,
Where ever since I've lived my dreams;
Where I've swayed afraid
In a nightmare conceived
Of a long reaching staircase
And wide huge angry rooms of space;
Where a sled drives through snow
Repetitively in a place I know;
Where a peaceful fence slopes
And running round a corner my dog speaks.

Wonder if I've laid my dreams
At last, for the old house is
Of its old nobility stripped.
Silent, bare, like a rotted grave-post
It stands. The worst
Is that it's shrunk.
In my mind of childhood I'd made it grow
Larger each year
Like my grandfather's peaches
And cherries, remembered from Luxembourg.
My aunts took him back once
Partly to stop his stories of the immense
Size of the fruit, to make him see them as they were,
Knotted and tiny and imperfect.

Wonder if it were wise to go
And enter square boxed toy rooms
And pass white small unfamiliar doors
Laid out in the same proper pattern. But so

Diminished! Up the short staircase whose walls
Grew in while I was not
There to watch. The falling dust
Smothers old loved cats and dogs
And pet crows that raced
And flew in the sun and gloom
Of my life a short while ago.

For a Father

I remember you in various ways;
The picture I have of you of those days
Differs perhaps from what you'd think it is.
Living is an unprobed game that children play
Since everyone else is doing it too.
You sat on the house's top above three stairways,
Your skin caging the sun with brassed felicity,
And spoke to me father's counsel to which I gave little mind,
Though admiring your glad attitude and being
Sure that the world was firm, since you held
Its reins so exceeding well. The smoke
Had gone from your cold clenched cigar; the wood
Of the orange crate was hot to touch; in back

Of you the iron grill was flooded by a trumpet vine;
The tropical blooms hid clustering from
The sun which was stamped with your name,
Which belonged I knew to you.
That was one thing, the sun; another was
Your voice humming as you descended uncounted stairs
To where the rest of us were at table.
Two mad beautiful Irish setters howling joy
Prefaced your arrival. A song had begun lusty
When you reached the second staircase; it might be,
"Everybody works at our house but my old man!"
The faces in the room went wheeling to your voice. Then
Your affection for night, your walking through it,
Into its blackness where occasionally glowed
One evening star like a tiny sun
Or the beginning moon like a cobweb looped
Or an old sated one in a blue blaze.
For these thanks: the globe and bugle blooms, the red dogs
And song, and the night which I hold on temporary loan.

At Twenty
(To My Son)

The foreign soil is dusted on your shoes,
You, these many months gone, returned.
The arrogance of conquest is in your stance
As you hurl the door to and enter my domain.
Your fierce voice startles, used to a small son
Soberly erecting erector sets, not even swearing,
Conscientious, religious, within my hearing,
A gentle child! And I employing strong words at times
In a temper, being amazed and thinking you tender
And alien. You were a still boy, who now come
To my room, with a loud sound like laughter. Why, I wonder,
Can I scarcely touch your fresh hard face? Stranger!

This evening I glance across to where in a chair
Your cradled guitar makes odd tunes from some land
Where women shield their faces and men go hand in hand,
And you tear open black figs large as oranges,
The pink flesh hot and sweet and sensuous.
You have lifted veils; you have with those men
Taken wine resinous, half-warm. There is brine
In your new beard, sinewy your different hand.
In the shadow your mouth glints telling of a dragon
And mermaids, of swine to men and men to swine.
Rocked on my knees in a fever were you once mine?
With mouth then like a flower from which now I turn?

You do not know nor ever shall, tall one,
How frequently to my angel I mention
Your name in a bargaining fashion. Let, I pray, this rebel son
Outlive me! no longer any visible part to him.

Someone Should Say It to You, Daughter

Someone should say it to you, daughter: love.
Daughter, I loved you when you were three
The way I loved the golden spaniel pup,
Who scampered sunny-tempered on the porch.
You never cried, you laughed;
You never walked, you ran;
You never liked, you loved;
You never spoke, you sang.

Someone should say it to you, daughter: love.
Daughter, I love you best now at nineteen,
The lines of worry there where you have frowned,
Your quiet way of going from a room.
You cry too much, you laugh too much,
You walk too much, and run;
You like too much, you love too much,
You speak too much, and sing.

Yesterday I saw in you no part of me,
Although I knew that you were of my blood
And had my smile and had my mother's eyes.
Sister, today you stood before the glass
And took the comb and ran it through your hair
And looked into your eyes and there saw me
And my mother and her mother and hers.
Let someone say it, daughter, sister: love.

Song for Sascha

I can't talk much with my grandson
He's eight hundred miles away
But I hear from his mother and father
That he said three words today

He put his socks in the fishbowl
And strawberry jam in his shoe
And the three words on his first birthday
Were *Mama* and *Teddy* and *Poo*

When Sascha and I met six months ago
And he laughed his belly laugh
I thought I'd love my grandson
Till the cow turned into a calf

Till the moon became a pumpkin
And butterflies changed into birds
And yesterday was tomorrow
And whistles were used for words

Till trees get up and dance around
And daisies begin to sing
And the North Star runs away to the south
And nothing is everything

Till questions turn into answers
And a coat becomes a hat
I'll still be loving Sascha
And nothing will ever change that

On Leaving My Six-day-old Grandson, Birch

A whippoorwill called in the dark
When I came on your birthday.
Birch, be a sound close to the house
While no one can find you.

A Luna moth hatched from the living-room
Wood box two weeks ago.
Birch, be a mystery no one can plumb
Coming from hidden places.

A quail covey whirred like a waterfall
Across the road down there.
Birch, be quick to be seen
And then to be gone.

Five baby wrens crowded last evening
On the porch rafters.
Birch, be a soft piping in golden air
Before ever going away.

All the azaleas are blazing in the
Greening wood about your home.
Birch, be fire within your life
Which is the leaves around you.

Freed

The old goose on the island on the pond
Had six goslings rolled up
Inside their casings like pretzels.
Today they chipped at the stone walls of their prison
And became released yellow skidding balls.
If they can elude the prowling raccoon and the fox
And those underwater dragons, the snapping turtles,
They will this fall skim screaming across the sky!

And O, my grandson was a prisoner as well.
He rolled and kicked and beat upon the soft walls,
But could not cry out.
Then one day he took the long dive to freedom,
Dangerous, swimming the narrow channel,
But he made it, gasping as the journey ended
And air filled his lungs for the first time.
The lucky boy's voice was terrible to hear!

Amen

When the doctors managed to pull my mother round
And sent her back to us at ninety in the spring,
At first I thought it wrong because her mind
Is lost in the past, wandering
About the foreign land of her childhood,
Speaking the old-time tongue
Or explaining science to her students
Or reasoning out religion.

Miles away in another place her great-grandson
Is in his crib, his mind at eighteen months so young
There is nowhere for him to wander in,
No tongue to speak of gods or wars or home.
The birds are singing through the windows of spring
And in the garden flowers burst and bloom.
The sober eyes of my mother and my grandson
Follow the leaping sunrays through the room.

To a Step-Grandson One Hour of Age

This island, you said,
I'm leaving this island, you said,
And that is what you did,
Astonishing your young mother,
Standing in the golden sun,
Waving goodbye from the door,
Hearing your shout
As you reached the other shore.

This dark land, you said,
I've reached this dark land, you said,
And fell exhausted upon the sand,
Wept and slept,
Nostalgic already for your mother.
Later you will go around the bend of shore
And, surprising both of you, meet her
For the first time face to face.

Sonnet about My Daughter among the Flowers

Paula comes before them, sprinkling can in hand,
Trailing a hose, and all the petals start to turn,
Until the blooms are gazing where she stands,
Moody-faced, blue-jean clad, freckled, burned.

Paula somehow knows the feeling in their toes
For dampness now or dryness then, the urgent need
For long unhurried sleep. Somehow she knows
The little or great potential of each seed.

She hovers about the green growing things for hours,
Abstracted, surprised, stirred—Paula among the flowers.

From in the Dream
(For Barney)

Dear love, I said to you from in the dream,
Say what makes the willow tree so green,
Say what makes the light on pale skin gleam,
Say while we lie together in the dream.

Your mouth on mine I heard your heart repeat,
The willow's roots are long and dark and sweet,
The pale light is the space where voices meet,
Then where is love? I heard my quick heart beat.

Love, you said, is of its own self wove,
It is not us; there is no act to prove.
In its green time this thing will choose to move
And then into the dream stood love.

The Invisible Animals

The woods is a white map of tracks in snow.
The rabbit, the fox, the squirrel, the shrew.
The waddling possum's thumbprint there,
The miniscule handy hands of the coon,
Squiggles of bugs and crawling things,
Here went the bounding Whitetail deer,
Here the singing Whitefoot mouse.
I'm beginning to see the invisible animals.

Once, it's true, I saw a pronged buck
And a winter ago a doe or its shadow.
I've never seen a rabbit, just its mark
And the only possum was in my trap,
Fat and sleepy and glutted on sweet corn,
Not ambling along, humming a song.
But it's out of its hibernation hole,
There's its thumbprint and its four toes.

They are furtive and silent and move in dark,
Their thoughts their own and not to be shared.
A long single line crosses the frozen pond
Where Red Reynard glided in a dainty ballet,
His belly ready to compromise. If not the
Rabbit, take the mouse or the shrew, any of them
Will do, nibbling at their sticks and twigs,
Their eyes alive with apprehension.

See those heart-shaped prints of hoofs
There on each side of the six-foot fence?
The rocking-horse gaited deer were here.
Why won't he come like the unicorn and
Let me reach up to stroke his horns
And see the warm eyes of the skittery does?
Elusive, aloof and shy, they bounded by
And took the fence with their tails held high.

I'm beginning to see the invisible animals.
The slinking weasel fitting its hind feet
Into its front, nosy and loping and doubling
Back to munch on whatever made that crawling
Track that wound through the thicket, maybe
A cricket or else an elf-bug on a mission.
The invisible animals are crowding the path
They don't make a sound in their passage.

We are walking unafraid of each other!
Like a Fairy Tale the Whitefoot mouse sings
His song to the fox, the rabbit lopes with
The weasel, the possum and coon are arm in arm,
The shrew, the crawling ones, hustle along.
The high-stepping stag leads the way,
His sloe-eyed does are nudging my elbow.
Listen! I am seeing the invisible animals!

Country People Are Less Alone than Others

Country people are less alone than others,
Because when living becomes too much to endure
Any more and the burden of infinity presses,
They turn to the animals who are always there.

The sweet-breathed ponderous silken-hided cows
Stand in their stalls like monuments of serenity
To young women wounded by quarrel or bereavement
Or conscious suddenly of the lost hope of eternity.

The old ones pushed aside in haste or hate by kin,
Go to speak to amber eyes of growing beasts
And lean upon the shaggy manes and strong-veined necks
Until themselves are vested again with strength.

Children and young men making pride their religion,
Cannot therefore weep in the sight of day;
Only in the hot dark stall where the animal stands
Can they become assuaged and begin again to pray.

Poems to the Dog, Gustav

I

Look, the dog's name is Gustav
And his eyes are golden; he is huge,
Shaggy-coated and mustached,
Gray-bearded and beetle-browed.

Look, he is noble and responsible;
If I move about the house in the small hours,
His dark padding follows me;
Weary, he cannot lie and dream upstairs.

Look, he does not bore me with discussions,
He does not insist that I listen,
He does not mind whether I weep or shout.
I call the dog, Gustav, marvelous!

I I

Little there is in me that comprehends
The riddle of this dog's devotion;
Ravished with love, he comes to gaze at me,
Enchanted if I turn to look at him.

When I pack my bags to make a trip,
He goes at once to sulk at top of stair;
If I rush to weep upon my bed,
He follows me to sigh and settle there.

Man has worn his gods out one by one,
Busy with his own destruction,
But golden-eyed Gustav has only to nudge my hand
And paradise is there at his command!

The Garden

It is summer and at the bottom of the hill
Lies my garden, hot and demanding.
The female peacock has not been seen for three weeks now;
She is either dead or nesting.
The male roams up and down our farm screaming
From every tree in the mornings;
In the afternoons he visits my garden
To pluck out every other sprouting bean
From the newly planted rows.
Our tulip tree was struck by lightning in the night
When the heavy oven of air was finally broken by thunder.

Every day is the same in this sweet summer;
The earth smells as it did in my childhood.
I wear but shirt and jeans nowadays;
My hands and bare feet will not any more scrub clean.
The hours swing like pendulums from the hot globe;
The sky stays blue and cloud shapes do not move.
Here the sunflowers soar, the cucumber scrambles past.
I bend into the knotted roots and tender leaves;
The joints of my back refuse to straighten again,
Except when the burning male peacock, like Icarus falling,
Goes beating and shrieking down from the tallest oak.

The Fable of the Dog and the Possum

Last night late in dark
We heard our great dog roar
And rush with heated bark
The garden to explore

The possum ambling there
Was caught in our dog's maw
Gave up forthwith the ghost
In the crunching jaw

Our dog in prideful lust
Paraded here and there
Until we said he must
For our disgust forebear

The possum in the morning light
Has himself taken away
And if I stand for dog or possum
I cannot say

In Time

Beneath the icy pond outside my window
Are eight half-frozen goldfish
Lying in formation, prepared to swim.
One is pale and speckled,
The other seven are carmine,
And all are glorious and held still in
time.

Within my window is an amaryllis.
Its tall leafless single stalk
Kept forging toward heaven,
Finally stopping to prepare to bloom.
All the glorious carmine buds
Are paused before their explosion in
time.

Night Riders

They only came out in the dark.
We knew they were there because of the minute
Squeak or shrilling sound somewhere between
A cricket and a field mouse,
And then they took off, two of them.
We knew they were bats because during the day
They folded their wings and crept in to rest
Behind a heavy painted board.
We moved it a bit and glimpsed them
Hanging by their tiny toes.

But at dark they hunted something, we supposed,
Because don't bats live on insects they find
In the air? What else would they be after
In our old cabin, swirling and flapping
And soaring and descending and squeaking
In the night over our bed? Was it pure joy?

Last week the cleaning lady found them
Behind their board. "They tried to get away,
But I knocked them down with the
Broomstick. I did them in for sure. I threw them
Out there. They won't bother you no more."
Two night riders grounded forever.

The Clown Prince

The Clown Prince, we call the peacock baby.
Our Princeling that we counted on
To run in spring with the three peahens.
His mother dead by the fox's deed,
Orphaned and raised with the chickens,
He starts when the speckled bantam calls her brood,
Rushes when the racy red cockerel sprints.
Bewildered, slim, gray-legged, he pecks in the sun,
His small crown elegant and erect.

The Clown Prince has no sign on him or notion within
Of the fabled tail his father and even the fox's meal wore.
The deprived trio of enormous hens don't know who he is,
Do not recognize the Princeling as some future sire of young,
High-crowned with six-foot spangled rainbowed arc.

And where does our baby spend his winter days,
But in the safety of the barn loft,
Roosting on the rafters along with the hens,
Scratching time away in the chaff of the floor.
And where are the wives that we arranged him for?
Why, high on the branch of a towering chestnut oak,
The falling snow covering them all night long,
Heavenly creatures far beyond the reach of the Clown Prince!

Walking the Dog

> *It is Sunday now, John, and all have gone to church. . . .*
> *I have come out in the new grass. Three or four hens have*
> *followed me and we sit side by side and while they crow and*
> *whisper, I'll tell you what I see today . . .*
>
>

—Emily Dickinson, letter to
John L. Graves, April 1856

Seeing is for Emily and me. With undaunted rapture
We attend to God, glorious in the treetops,
To the far-stretching hills, the hens in the pasture.

Smelling is for the dog. With down-looking ecstasy
He studies each footprint, man or beast, absorbed,
Pees where warranted, then kicks, abandoned, recklessly.

While major and minor poets tremble at visions above,
The dog examines the mystery beneath with calculating love.

Eulogy for a Crow

Judging by larger graver sorrows,
The loss to some may seem a paltry one,
But this morning when I opened my country door
My crow, William, lay like a small black stone,
Pierced by the horned owl's claw to the bone.

Needless death is a thing I ponder on,
For the owl by the death of William made no gain.
Is the lesson of the going of my cheerful bird
That one must learn by small to bear large pain
And so stand the deaths of all innocent men?

William, missed on my walks today and tomorrow,
Swift, light-bodied, talkative—small sorrow!

Your Dog

When you leave, your dog turns into a statue.
I call him from the low window,
But as soon as my back's turned, he's there again.
He will not eat his dinner.
He will not turn when I speak to him.
His eyes burn steadily upon the driveway.
When you arrive, they burst into flame
And the house, which has been holding its breath,
Sighs and is at ease again.

The Cat and the Chameleon

The marmalade cat lies on the bed with his white stomach up.
He purrs to himself in half-sleep.
The chameleon has lost most of its tail in the teeth
And lies green now in the leaves of the gardenia,
Panting a little in the yellow sunlight.
Four times now the cat has caught it, holding it
So that except for the partial tail loss there is no harm.

Always the cat comes by me, an eye in my direction,
So that I may witness his praise-worthy ways.
Four times I have grasped his scruff and shaken him
And put the long creature before him, saying, "No and no!"
Always the cat slants his eye at me and twitches his tail
And goes to lie on the bed, white stomach up, purring.

Despite all my protest never will the cat change his ways
And this is clear to purring cat, panting chameleon and me.

On Transplanting Two Rootbound Monarda Fistulosa
and One Cushion Spurge

The roots were like white wires wound round and round,
When I turned the black plastic pots upside down
And the dry bit of falling powdered dirt was brown
And the three little plants made never a sound.

But I knew their feelings, what was going on,
As I eased them into the garden's dark damp ground.
Freedom!

In the north of Thailand in the town of Chiang Mai,
Near the Inn of Wiang on the way to Chiang Rai,
Where the Golden Triangle and Burma and Laos lie,
A street seller comes with her basket piled high

With wicker cages where silent birds lie that you buy
And release soaring and chittering into the sky.
Freedom!

Psalm to a Guinea Pig Less than One Day Old

Last night the guinea pig who lives in our kitchen
Gave birth to three, as beautiful as she, young!
I have the smallest in my palm,
Who surveys me, remains calm
And attends to my guinea pig psalm:

Oh little beast, oh mystery!
Smooth of coat and bright of eye,
Seventy days in the womb you lay
And then sprang forth so splendidly
And fearless about the world began to roam!

This is no poem, but an encomium.

The Killer

O, blood on the snow and the circling tracks
And the carcass of the hamstrung young buck deer.
The bare frozen trees with their unborn flowers laden
All were witness to the moonlight-dancing farmer's dog.
The icy floor beneath is the roof to the bedrooms
Of all the underground creatures who heard it happen,
The stomping trancèd deer falling under the growls
Of the one who hangs his head now, licking the farmer's hand.
Insects in their winter shrouds are refusing to move,
The snow is hurrying to cover the murder over,
Falling forever from the darkening March skies.
Some say there will not even be a spring this year!

Karma
(For Dr. Haruo Ezaki of Hiroshima)

The woodchuck has fulfilled his karma.
He wandered here after snow peas and new lettuce
And now in his burrow, elbows out, he resists
The pull on the rope attached to the trap
That holds his toes.

A Buddhist friend is visiting from Japan
And shows none of my alarm.
The woodchuck has been advancing step by step
To the trap that holds his toes.
It is his karma.

To a Dog Whose Mistress Is in Europe for a Month

The absence of the voice, the familiar flame—
He cannot name what it is, but it is there.
When a strange car arrives and brakes outside,
He rises quickly, remembering how she came
And walked and called and was a part of him.

Strong, a little thin, his brown eyes warm,
The dog survives the inner uncomprehended storm.

The Rape of the Garden

The little pear tree stands in shock, stripped.
The nectarine is girdled and gone.
Not one bean is left to report the story,
How the eggplants were dragged up to lie with roots exposed,
When the barbarian cows broke down the gate and crowded in.

Did okra blossom here with elegant tulip petals?
Did carrots stand in a lush and ferny row,
Swiss chard thrive in verdant profusion?
All have disappeared into the drooling mouths
Of the satisfied beasts who stand heaving, mournful-eyed,
Watching me counting what they have left,
The ragged tomato rows, melons and squashes disdained,
The green-laced untouched cucumber patch, red-gold pumpkins,
A twelve-foot prickly expanse of zucchini,
Where no cow would place hoof or tongue.

There are the torn hooks, where the fall-dizzy ones leaned
And when no one saw, rammed down the gate,
Their veneer of civilization shed,
Primeval joy on the loose—the cows in my garden.

The Message

The pink spider that was in our bathroom yesterday
Was so tiny you would not believe it.
There was only the one swinging across on its trapeze
And climbing hand over hand to the ceiling light,
All the time looking me squarely in the eye.

It was not there today and no one has been cleaning up.
Did it emerge from some egg sac?
Where are the others? Where the mother?
Or is it a message—
A small delicate dazzling message that I understand?

The Stroke

A blow is what it was,
An intruder whacking you on your side.
Slam! So you fell
And crawled across the kitchen floor,
Heading for a solid rug to grip.

(You'd been standing at the counter
At the morning paper, while I shopped.)

Slam!

You sighed, your voice different,
"I think I slipped."
(Telling me when I blew in and stared.)
"You should never leave me.
I think I killed the cat."
(Who gazed, mild, from the corner.)

The sudden soft silent intruder within yourself
Striking. Slam!
The stroke.

Poem for My Husband on His Birthday
Which He Didn't Quite Make

Now that you are gone you are coming into my dreams
In an ordinary way your hand on my hand
And nothing dramatic and moving into a problem
Affecting you and asking my opinion
Your presence strong and amiable and shouldering
Others out of the dream and it was wonderful
And I thought waking he isn't gone then
And I lay wondering in the dark warm of the bed

A Pure Act

The dog has brought me a ball
And the heartache is gone
And did not drift away
But sped and had not been

His eyes are dark and brilliant
And burn where he stands
In pure dog pleasure
Holding a dilapidated small
Rather sacred and holy ball
Which he wishes me to throw

Widow's Sonnet

The widow is standing there in the moonlit night;
She is watching herself to see what she will do.
The pain had been dark and hard and he was right
To leave her to live alone and would she be blue?

In his death in the hospital bed, he had been pale;
She'd been stopped in her tracks at the tyranny of his love.
But the terror was gone and the cry in the night, instead
Wind in trees, fruits, flowers, the moon above!

Her foot reaches out for his in the bed in the night;
Her friends are cross because she does not weep.
The widow is fine, she is going to be all right;
The ecstasy came sudden and thudding and deep,

And when loneliness knocked, she went to open the door
And all alone she danced across the floor!

Widow's Sonnet #2

Do you come back to see if it's like before,
The way you wanted, lamps polished and new shades,
The garden aglow, a friend standing at the door,
Floors scrubbed, most of the bills paid?

The unfolding roses are on the counter there,
That you used to present from the local grocery place,
Because they were cheaper than the florist's fare
And still are—apricot and yellow—in your vase,

The one you bought in Taormina, of Italian blue.
Do you come back in a mild and gentle way
Not to protest or remonstrate, that would not do,
But to see if all's well as we agreed that day

When you gave me the news and your blue eyes smiled
And we knew that we still had a little while?

The Widow's Lover

He came out of the past remembering
And she remembered too
And it was a different rapture than expected,
For having been completely accustomed
To a perfect rhythm of adoration
And the combination of his body and her body
Over all those years, he was quite new
And a little astonishing,
The last *he* being the lover,
But he would not touch her against her wish,
His pleasure being kindness to her
And she was helpless in the candlelight
Amid the wine and the coffee and the words
And the male scent of musk,
Unused to preliminaries because of
The years of marriage and that ritual
Of her body and that other body
And a quite different rapture from this rapture.

Widow's Elegy

*I spend so much time alone that silence has
become a habit.*
　　　　　　　　—Beryl Markham,
　　　　　　　　West With the Night

Since your heart beat ever slower and then stopped,
And became silent, the house is spirit-filled.
The Mexican mask and the Japanese wedding robes
Have your hands on them and know it. The amphora
You lifted from the sea floor, the stones brought
From the Great Wall to remember the Long Walk,
All are yours in silence, hanging or lying there.

Since your laugh became a smile and then a word
And became silent, the air of the house clings.
In the yard the birds gather at the feeders,
The trees continue to be trees, the flowers flowers,
The tomatoes climb their trellises and Sweet Peas.
The moon hovers over all in rapturous splendor
And your presence is once more known to your friends.

You ranged in your curious way about the world
With camera and pen and notebooks and wives at heel,
And never believed that you'd seen or done enough,
Even dying, planning your next adventurous trip and
In your last day but one you composed a poem and
Cried with delight, "What satisfaction that was!"
While all about your silence was beginning to begin.

Praise with a Lament

The bell rings, the heart beats,
The tree once in bud blooms. Lament.
Standing in the doorway
With the rain wet on the street,
The scent of spring on the air. Lament.

And yet praise.
Driven by life and the circles,
The patterns of work, of love,
Praise the ending.
In time it will be over and rest.

Heat and stillness. No movement.
The bell sound lingers, the sun broods,
The tree stands unseen.
The door is closed.
Praise and lament.

Acknowledgments

The following poems first appeared in *The Unicorns* (New York: Dial Press, 1965), © Helga Sandburg: "The Accident"; "The Age of the Flower"; "Airmail in Summer"; "All Praise to the Virtue Purity"; "Am I Waiting for a Knock upon the Door?"; "At Twenty"; "The Ballad of Woman"; "Bravery"; "The Calf of the Black Cow"; "The Childe to the Tower Came"; "Destiny"; "The Giraffe"; "I Am Walking through Rooms"; "I'm Trying to Learn How to Die"; "The Importance of Mirrors"; "In My Room Your Red Roses Are Unbeautifully Dying"; "It Is April!"; "Let Us Suffer Alone, Lover"; "Lyric" (previously titled "Dust"); "On War"; "Sin"; "Someone Should Say It to You, Daughter"; "Sometimes I Feel the Envious Dead Crowd Near"; "The Unclasping"; "Visit."

The following poems first appeared in *To a New Husband* (Cleveland: World Publishing Company, 1970), © Helga Sandburg: "Country People Are Less Alone than Others"; "Dover Beach the Second"; "The Killer"; "Poems to the Dog, Gustav"; "Psalm to a Guinea Pig Less than One Day Old" (previously titled "Ode to a Guinea Pig . . .").

"Amen" first appeared in *Passage II* (River Grove, Ill.: Triton College, 1976). "Cantata for Two Lovers" first appeared in Louis Untermeyer, *An Uninhibited Treasury of Erotic Poetry* (New York: Delacorte, 1963). "Close the Door Quietly" (previously titled "The Visit") first appeared in *The New York Times* (1967). "Eulogy for a Crow" first appeared in *The Ladies Home Journal* (October 1969). "For a Father" (previously titled "Poems for a Father, I") first appeared in *Sweet Music* (New York: Dial Press, 1963), © Helga Sandburg. "In Time" first appeared in *Cricket* (1994) and is reprinted with permission. "The Middle of Time" first appeared in *The Chicago Tribune Magazine* (July 7, 1968). "Murder on the Table Top" first appeared in *The Worm Runner's Digest* 8 (November 1966). "On Transplanting Two Rootbound Monarda Fistulosa and One Cushion Spurge" first appeared in *Blue Unicorn* 13 (October 1989) and is reprinted with permission. "The Silence" first appeared in *Passage II* (River Grove, Ill.: Triton College, 1975). "Song for Sascha" and "Sonnet about My Daughter among the Flowers" first appeared in *The Ladies Home Journal* (October 1969). "The Teenagers" first appeared in *Hawk & Whippoorwill* 2 (Spring 1961). "Three Serpents in a Well in a Field" first appeared in *The Literary Review* (Autumn 1966). "To a Dog Whose Mistress Is in Europe for a Month" (previously titled "Poem for a Dog . . .") first appeared in *The Chi-*

Index of Titles

The Age of the Flower
was composed in Linotype-Hell Minion
using Aldus PageMaker 5.0 for Windows
at The Kent State University Press;
printed by sheet-fed offset
on Glatfelter 60-pound Natural acid-free stock,
notch case bound with 88-point binder's boards
in G.S.B. Natural book cloth,
and wrapped with dustjackets printed in
two colors on 80-pound Cross Pointe Passport stock
by Thomson-Shore, Inc.;
designed by Will Underwood;
and published by

THE KENT STATE UNIVERSITY PRESS
KENT, OHIO 44242